Exercises for Charles Duhigg's
Supercommunicators

Exercises for Reflection,
Processing, and Practising the Lessons

 BIG ACTION BOOKS

BigActionBooks.com

Contents

Claim your free bonus

There's a free bonus waiting for you as thanks for picking up this exercise book. We think you'll like it. Inside, you'll find a list of the most impactful self development books from this year, including:

- Top books for self-growth and mindfulness
- Top books for financial growth
- Top books for relationships (including yourself)
- Top books for productivity and "Getting Things Done"

We hope they provide a little inspiration for you - and perhaps some new discoveries.

To get your free bonus, scan the QR code below or visit BigActionBooks.com/bonus.

Scan to get your free bonus

Introduction

Master the tools of communication to connect meaningfully with anyone.

WHY THIS EXERCISE BOOK?

You've read Charles Duhigg's fabulous book about how to understand the expertly-observed nuances of communication, and take your own to the next level. Now it's time to actually *practice* it - write; journal; put the lessons in motion.

This exercise book was created as a **faithful friend** to Charles Duhigg's "Supercommunicators". While reading the book, we found ourselves wishing for a place where we could write, process and practise the book's exercises in a constructive, concise way. There are so many actionable takeaways - but there isn't much space to actually write in the book itself. Instead, we found ourselves cobbling notes together in various places - notebooks, journals, pieces of paper - all of which would eventually get lost, or at the very least, not be helpful in putting the lessons into practice. That's how this book was born.

HOW TO USE THIS EXERCISE BOOK

This exercise book is like a faithful friend to Supercommunicators. In it, you'll find exactly what's advertised: dozens of exercises based on the book, summarised and formatted, with space to answer.

- Dozens of exercises based on Supercommunicators, extracted into one single place
- Space to write under each exercise
- Lists, ruled lines and space for you to answer, journal and reflect
- Clearly organised and well-formatted so it's easy to follow

In each section, we've extracted the main premise of the exercise, and then added space to respond and practise the lessons. This may come in the format of a table to fill in, space to free-write, or other exercise methods to provide space for reflection. You'll also notice the "Parts" and "Chapters" referenced in the book, so you can easily find the section if you need to look back on it for further context.

If you want to not only read about how to become an expert communicator, and connect effortlessly with others in work and in life - but also put the lessons into practice - this exercise book, as well as your own dedication, will help you do just that.

Enjoy, and thank you.
Let's dive in!

* Please note: This is an unofficial exercise book for Supercommunicators to help motivated do-ers process the lessons from this fantastic book. It is not created by or associated with Charles Duhigg in any official way.

Chapter 1: The Matching Principle

The Yasmins In Your Life

The author takes us through a journey of understanding the **Matching Principle** by beginning to narrate the story of a man named Lawler, who wanted to be admitted into the CIA.

When he was asked why, he replied that he wanted to do something meaningful with his life. Once he got accepted, he was taken through a year of training.

Apart from being taught how to pick locks, the training mostly included lessons on **how to be an effective communicator**. When Lawler got "deployed" in Europe one year later, his job was to recruit "spies", people who would provide him with valuable information.

After some failures, Lawler met a woman from the Middle East, Yasmin, and got off to a good start with her. But when he told his boss about her, he was instructed to tell Yasmin the truth. If she agreed to work with them, she had to know that she would work closely with the CIA.

When Lawler did that, Yasmin was terrified and walked away.

Lawler knew that he had to win her trust. To do so, **he had to connect with her**.

> **Note:** Throughout this exercise book, you'll see examples in some places, listed in *grey handwriting like this.* These are just to give you an idea of the kind of action points you might like to take - but feel free to use or ignore them as best suits your style. There are also some blank pages at the end of this exercise book for free-writing and journaling.

Your turn: What are the Yasmins in your life, the people you need to connect with? Why?

Your "Yasmins"	Your Why
A colleague I work with who lives abroad.	*To produce better quality work in a shorter time.*

Factors Affecting Communication

What makes us click with others?

As humans, we crave to connect with others but that's not always easy to do. Sometimes it happens naturally while other times we leave an interaction with other people feeling drained or disappointed.

The factors affecting communication are virtually unlimited, but some major factors include:

- Tone of voice
- Body posture
- How you speak
- How you listen
- How open you are with your vulnerabilities

To connect with others, we need to achieve *neurological synchronisation,* which basically means we need to align our brains and bodies with them.

More on this in a bit. For now, flip to the next page and answer a few questions.

How do you usually speak? Fast or slow?

_____

_____

Are you a good listener or do you keep interrupting others?

_____

_____

How do you think you sound when you speak?

_____

_____

Do you feel comfortable exposing a few vulnerabilities about yourself if others do the same first?

_____

_____

Are you usually aware of your body's posture around others?

_____

_____

3 Conversations

There are essentially 3 types of conversations we have with others:

1. What's this really about?
2. How do we feel?
3. Who are we?

These conversations are associated with 3 mindsets:

1. Decision-making mindset.
2. Emotional mindset.
3. Social mindset.

Here's one rule to remember:

- Miscommunication happens when we have conversations taking place on different mindsets.

Each mindset can be uncovered by asking 3 questions regarding the other person:

1. Do they want to be helped? = Decision-making mindset = What's this really about?
2. Do they want to be hugged? = Emotional mindset = How do we feel?
3. Do they want to be heard? = Social mindset = Who are we?

Your turn: Recall the last long conversation you had with another person and fill in the table below.

Conversation Content	Conversation Mindset.	Did I match it?
My father was mostly rumbling about how my mother sticks her nose in his business.	It was on the Emotional Mindset. He just wanted to lay it.	Probably not. I tried to give him advice, which touched on the decision-making mindset.

One More Dinner With Yasmin and The Matching Principle

The author concludes the story about Lawler and Yasmin. Lawler convinced her to have one more dinner.

Yasmin was nervous, so Lawler was trying to crack some jokes and lighten the mood. However, it wasn't working. Then, Lawler got lucky as he started sharing a story that accidentally matched Yasmin's mood.

This helped him connect with Yasmin and Lawler only figured out what he did later in his life. Like a miracle happened, Yasmin agreed to work with the CIA and provide them with information.

This uncovers the **Matching Principle**, which consists of 2 steps:

1. Understand the other person's mindset.
2. Then match it.

Silently ask yourself:

- **What conversation are we having?**

Loudly ask others:

- What do you want to talk about?

Your turn: Follow the author's suggestion and prepare for your next conversation by setting your intention.

What's the next important conversation you are going to have?

With my spouse about who does the most chores around the house, which is me.

What do you want to say?

That he/she has to help more with the chores because I'm doing almost everything.

How do you want to say it?

If we share the chores equally, that buys us more time to spend together and have fun.

Chapter 2: Every Conversation Is A Negotiation

Wants And Rules

We said many things about conversations, but how do we decide what to talk about and in what tone to talk about it?

The author introduces us to a term researchers call "*quiet negotiation*". This refers to a push and pull happening between people until they unconsciously (most of the time) agree on what to talk about.

There are two components that really guide us in picking which conversations to have or not have:

1. What everybody wants.
2. The rules for making a decision together.

Can you recall a conversation from your life where you clearly knew the rules of reaching a decision with other people?

A business meeting about an ad campaign. Deciding if we would stop or keep the campaign running would depend on its performance until that day, facts and numbers.

_____

_____

_____

_____

Real Wants VS Underlying Wants

The first step to figuring out what's it about is to recognize that every conversation is a negotiation. Here it's very important to have clarity on your real wants.

Some of the wants we think we have seem obvious but there are underlying wants as well. Follow the example in the table below and try to think of 2 communications you are considering having, what's the want behind them, and if there is an underlying want somewhere deep inside of you.

Communication	Want	Real Want
Ask my teacher if I can do some extra work to get some extra credit	Be top of the class this school/college year	Make my parents admire me and see my worth

Preparing For A Conversation

Expanding more on the above, the author suggests preparing for your next conversations.

Fill in the tips provided by the author as you read them to prepare for an awesome start to your next conversations.

What are two topics you might discuss? (Being general is okay: TV shows you like)

_____

_____

_____

_____

What is one thing you hope to say?

_____

_____

_____

_____

What is one question you will ask?

_____

_____

_____

_____

If you can be even more specific, consider answering these questions as well:

What are two topics you most want to discuss?

_____

_____

_____

_____

What is one thing you hope to say that shows what you want to talk about?

_____

_____

_____

_____

What is one question you will ask that reveals what others want?

_____

_____

_____

_____

Others' Wants

In each communication, you are not alone. Other people participating in a form of communication have their own wants, which are not necessarily the same as yours.

To find out what they want, you need to take 2 steps:

1) Ask open-ended questions.

You can prepare these questions in advance, right now.

Asking about someone's beliefs or values.

How did you decide to become a teacher?

_____

_____

_____

_____

Asking someone to make a judgement.

Are you glad you went to law school?

_____

_____

_____

_____

Asking about someone's experiences.

What was it like visiting Europe?

_____

_____

_____

_____

This sums up the part of asking questions. But what do you do with their answers?

2) You listen closely, noticing what clues they give back to you.

Below we will provide a few important things to pay attention to. Study these items and return here after one of your conversations to check the ones that appeared during your interaction.

- ☐ Do they lean toward you?
- ☐ Do they make eye contact?
- ☐ Do they smile?
- ☐ Do they backchannel ("Interesting," "Hmm"), or interrupt you?

Those are signals they want to accept your invitation. Interruptions, usually mean people want to add something.

- ☐ Do they become quiet?
- ☐ Do their expressions become passive, their eyes fixed somewhere besides your face?
- ☐ Do they seem overly contemplative?
- ☐ Do they take in your comments without adding thoughts of their own?

These are signals that someone is declining your invitation and wants to talk about something else, in which case, you need to keep searching and experimenting to learn what everyone wants.

Rules Of Common Decision-Making

After getting a clearer image of their wants, it's time to find out how they make their decisions.

The author differentiates between two kinds of logic for making decisions:

1. **Contrasting costs to benefits**. This is all about facts and rationality.
2. **Using the logic of similarities**. A person recalls similar past experiences and unconsciously asks "What does someone like me do in these situations?"

Apart from the above, the author also talks about **transforming conflict**. Here's how to do it:

- Introduce topic variations.
- For example, let's assume you are negotiating to get a raise but your manager says there is no way she can do that because of X reason. You suggest a variation. Maybe getting one extra day off per month without cutting your salary down.

A negotiation doesn't mean that somebody has to lose. It could be a win-win situation if you get creative with it.

Your turn: You need to answer this question:

- Is this a practical discussion or an empathetic one?

There is only one way to do it. Start experimenting with new topics and approaches until something useful is revealed. We can figure out which new topics and approaches might be fruitful by paying attention to a few things.

Study the items provided below and return here to check if any of them appear after you conduct your next conversation.

- ☐ **Has someone told a story or made a joke?** If so, they might be in an empathetic logic of similarities mindset. In this mindset, people aren't looking to analyse; they want to share, relate, and empathize.
- ☐ **Are they talking about plans and decisions, or evaluating options?** If so, they might be in a more practical logic of costs and benefits mindset, and you're better off getting analytical yourself.
- ☐ **Listen for attempts to change the topic**. People tell us what they want to discuss through their sudden shifts. If someone asks the same question in different ways, or if they abruptly introduce a new subject, it's a sign they want to add something to the table.
- ☐ **Experiment**. Tell a joke or ask an unexpected question. Introduce a new idea. Try interrupting. Watch to see if they play along. If they do, they are showing you how they'd like this conversation to continue

Chapter 3: The Listening Cure

3 Magic Questions

A bunch of hedge fund managers attended a conference in order to hear Professor Epley telling them how to become better listeners. They were surprised to learn that **becoming a better listener involves becoming more emotional and answering the "How do we feel?" question.**

Research has shown that **emotion helps us connect**, but how do we elicit emotions? To elicit emotional answers from others, we need to ask questions that refer to one of 3 areas:

1. Their beliefs.
2. Their values.
3. Meaningful experiences of theirs.

Emotional contagion is real but to trigger it, we need to use vulnerability on both ends. We need to become vulnerable as much as the other party. We need reciprocity in vulnerability.

If they become vulnerable, we become vulnerable as well. If we want them to open up, then we become vulnerable first and wait for them to reciprocate.

If only one party is vulnerable, then something is not flowing as it should.

Professor Epley has come up with 3 questions that help people connect deeply. Answer these questions on the next page as if we were asking you. Then, try to remember these questions and use them in your own life when there is solid ground for them. Preferably, you would use them with people you don't know very well but you share a common goal with, not complete strangers.

If a crystal ball could tell you the future, would you want to know?

_____

_____

_____

_____

For what do you feel most grateful?

_____

_____

_____

_____

Can you describe a time you cried in front of another person?

_____

_____

_____

_____

Deeper Questions

When you don't know people very well, or they are a bit distant, you don't want to ask very deep questions straight ahead but you still want to ask questions that elicit emotions.

To do this, you can **reshape standard questions into deeper questions.** Follow the example in the table below to replace standard questions with more meaningful ones.

Standard Question	Deeper Question
Where do you live?	*What do you like about your neighbourhood?*

Chapter 4: How Do You Hear Emotions No One Says Aloud?

Non-Linguistics VS Language

The author mentions that we are good at "reading" non-verbal cues when we are babies but we lose that ability as we grow because we put more of our attention on what's spoken.

Words carry information and it gradually becomes easier to focus on them rather than non-verbal communication.

How good are you at reading non-verbal cues? Rate yourself on a scale from 0 (absolute noob) to 10 (expert).

- ☐ 0
- ☐ 1
- ☐ 2
- ☐ 3
- ☐ 4
- ☐ 5
- ☐ 6
- ☐ 7
- ☐ 8
- ☐ 9
- ☐ 10

Connecting Over Laughter

A psychiatrist at NASA was faced with a difficult challenge. He had to find a few astronauts suitable for 1-year long trips to space. The expert, a man named McGuire, knew that he had to rely on people who were emotionally intelligent.

This realisation had come to him as evidence provided by previous missions of shorter timeframes, where astronauts had failed to keep themselves together.

As McGuire went through the interviews, he wasn't certain about the candidates who were really competent and those who just faked it.

Hoping to assist himself with these important assessments, McGuire decided to play some tapes from older interviews in order to look for clues. Suddenly, he found what he was looking for: Some candidates **laughed** differently.

As researchers have found, **we use laughter to connect**. The critical component to look for is **the intensity of the laughter**.

The intensity needs to be in symphony. Here are a few examples:

- You laugh hard while the other person just smiles. There is no connection or intention to connect.
- They laugh in a medium intensity and you match that intensity yourself. There is an intention to connect.

If we agree to laugh in similar ways, it probably means we want to connect. This is what McGuire used in his own interviews to determine which candidates inherently placed emphasis on their emotional skills.

Your turn: Use this knowledge to estimate if you are connected to some people in your life.

Person	Estimation
My thesis program roommate.	Not connected. We don't even laugh together.

Mood And Energy

A ninja trick that will enable you to connect with others is to **notice their mood and energy, and then match it.**

Here's what to look for:

1. Mood can be positive or negative.
2. Energy can be high or low.

There are 4 possible combinations of mood and energy:

1. Positive mood, high energy.
2. Positive mood, low energy.
3. Negative mood, high energy.
4. Negative mood, low energy.

NOTE: You don't have to hate life if they do. You are matching their way of communication, not their content, beliefs, or values.

Your turn: Do some people in your life usually fall under certain categories?

Person	Mood	Energy
My manager	*Negative*	*High*

Chapter 5: Connecting Amid Conflict

Conflicts

It appeared to be just another day in high school until Melanie Jeffcoat noticed her fellow students running scared.

A shooter had opened fire, killing one teacher and two of her classmates.

Later in her life, Melanie became a mother. Unfortunately, another incident took place at her daughter's school. The school was placed in lockdown as they suspected a shooter.

These experiences created anxiety in Melanie and she found herself always looking for exits when she was in the movies with her daughters in case a shooter would burst in.

She decided that she had to do something about it and joined a group to protest against guns. That would lead her to engage in various conflicts later on.

But what is a conflict?

It is simply **a contradiction of beliefs, values, opinions, etc**.

Let's start building from here.

Your turn:

What was the last conflict you remember having with another person?

_____

_____

_____

_____

Was the conflict resolved? How did it end up?

_____

_____

_____

_____

A Fight Consists Of 2 Conflicts

When we get caught up in a conflict against others, we usually get defensive. We believe that when we are in a conflict, we need to do everything we can to win.

However, researchers have found that **the best thing to do first is to understand why this conflict is taking place**.

To gain more insights into a conflict, you need to remember that a fight usually consists of 2 conflicts:

1. A surface-level conflict.
2. An emotional conflict.

Example:

- Two partners argue about having a second child. One of them wants it but the other doesn't.
- The surface-level conflict is, obviously, whether to have the child or not.
- The emotional conflict can be different for each partner, such as having to make more sacrifices, having to prioritise family over career, etc.

Your turn: Recall the conflict you wrote in the previous exercise or a different one.

What was the surface-level conflict?

_____

_____

_____

_____

What was the emotional conflict?

_____

_____

_____

_____

Talk About Emotions

Most people neglect to talk about their emotions during conflict because they have no idea this is an important part of reaching a resolution.

Although you or the other person might not change your mind or agree on something, **talking about emotions will at least stop you from arguing pointlessly**.

What do you associate expressing emotions during a conflict with?

- ☐ Expressing emotions during a conflict is a weakness.
- ☐ Expressing emotions during a conflict is mature.
- ☐ Expressing emotions during a conflict is pointless.
- ☐ Expressing emotions during a conflict will make me appear less masculine.
- ☐ Expressing emotions during a conflict will make me appear unstable.
- ☐ They will never understand anyway.
- ☐ I don't want to open up to my enemy.
- ☐ They never listen to anything.

Emotional Similarities

Melanie attended an event which was kind of different. The organisers invited people with different views on gun ownership to discuss their opinions.

But before they would do so, the organisers would train them to use a specific technique, more on that in a bit.

The goal was for people of opposing beliefs and values to emotionally understand their "rivals".

Melanie heard a woman telling her story. The woman owned a gun and never slept without it next to her bedstand. Her reason for doing so was an incident that happened to a relative of hers.

An intruder broke into her house and behaved aggressively. The woman at the event wouldn't like to find herself in a similar situation, so she got a gun as a means of protection.

Melanie understood that owning a gun was a way for her to feel safe. That was an emotional need that Melanie could relate to very well.

Your turn: Think of some people you are often caught up in conflicts with and see if there are any emotional similarities between you and them.

Person	Emotional Similarities
My dad	-Craving for attention -Proving our worth -Feeling like life owes us.

Diffusing Conflicts

There is a specific method for diffusing conflicts. Thankfully, it's easy to follow:

1. Ask the other person open-ended questions to make them open up.
2. Repeat what they said in your own words.
3. Ask them "Am I right?" or "Did I get it right?"

Remember, this doesn't guarantee that you and the other party will reach an agreement but the conflict will be diffused.

You will get a better understanding of their beliefs and they will better understand you.

Human beings have reasons for doing what they do and the trick to uncover those reasons is to focus on emotions when things get emotional.

By the way, we are not trying to shift from the decision-making mindset to the emotional mindset, we are matching the other person's mindset.

Your turn: You don't have to be in a conflict to practise this skill. Grab your phone and call someone (could be someone you need to call anyway).

1. Ask questions.
2. Repeat what they say.
3. Ask if you got it right.

Notes/Reflections:

_____

_____

_____

_____

Happy Wife, Happy Life?

A group of researchers was determined to find out what separates a happy marriage from an unhappy one. They interviewed more than 1,000 couples and were surprised to have most of their assumptions busted.

What they came to understand was that everything boils down to **control**.

As they noticed, unhappy couples tried to control one another when they argued.

On the contrary, happy couples tried to control:

1. **Themselves**: They made a step back or took a breath.
2. **The environment**: "Let's have this conversation in a place we feel safe".
3. **The conflict**: "Let's stop arguing if we realise that we switch topics".

This creates a feeling that we share control over something. **I am not trying to control you but rather control this conflict with you.**

Your turn: Based on everything you've learned, do your best to fill in the following table.

Behaviour	Happy Couples	Unhappy Couples
Control	Themselves	Their partner
Tone of voice		
Do they ask questions?		
Do they listen?		
Mood?		
Energy?		

Chapter 6: Our Social Identities Shape Our Worlds

Your Social Identity

Jay Rosenbloom had an M.D. and a Ph.D but when he became a working doctor, he knew that he would perform procedures that older doctors weren't in the mood to perform.

When Rosenbloom started giving vaccines to children, he didn't expect that many parents would oppose him.

Many parents seemed to believe that there was some kind of conspiracy going on. Vaccines would make their children prone to diseases, allowing big pharmaceuticals to sell more drugs and make more money.

Rosenbloom asked the older doctors for advice on how to convince these parents that the vaccines would help their children but nobody had an answer.

As academics developed an interest in studying this vaccine opposition phenomenon, they figured out that this ideology relates to the parents' **social identities**. They view themselves as the people who "don't want to be told what to do by the government".

The table on the next page presents some attributes that constitute our social identities. Fill your own social identity in as you understand it.

Attribute	Your Identity
Sexual Orientation	
Ethnicity	
Profession	
Income	
Status	
Gender	
Religion	
Age	

Tribes

The author explains the difference between personal identity and social identity.

- **Personal identity** = How I see myself.
- **Social identity** = How I see myself and how I think others see me as a member of tribes.

But what is a tribe? It can be anything that groups you together with other people. Here are a few examples:

1. The CrossFit gym where you workout with a certain group.
2. People who support the same NBA team as you.
3. The kids who are in the same group as you in summer camp.

The tribes we belong to affect how we behave and how we think. That happens because we need to reinforce our sense of belonging.

You see, we like more people who are like us and we expect them to like us back if we belong in the same tribe. The more exclusive or closely bonded a tribe is, the more powerful our connection becomes to its other members.

Your turn: List a few people you like or dislike from your life and write if they belong to the same tribe as you. Try to notice how the tribe dynamic affects your feelings toward them.

Person	Like or Dislike?	Same Tribe or Not?

Stereotype Effect - Part 1

A university professor noticed that black students and white females score less in math as compared to white male students.

To find out what was going on, or whose fault was this (for example, other professors with prejudices in their heads), the professor decided to conduct an experiment.

The students wrote two separate hard tests on short time limits. Time limits were important because the black students and the white female students underperformed in those. One of the tests was an English test while the other was a math test.

All students performed well in the English test while white male students performed better than the other target students in math.

The professor was able to pin down what happened. There was no prejudice when it came to English but there was a prejudice when it came to math, suggesting that white males do butter on that subject.

The white female students and the black students fell victim to that prejudice. As the professor noticed, they would waste time to double check their answers while also trying to figure out the answers to the next questions.

This was called the *Stereotype Effect*:

- **A pre-existing prejudice that applies to us, affects our behaviour.**

Stereotype Effect - Part 2

A group of researchers became interested in the Stereotype Effect and they decided to repeat the experiment.

However, they used a technique on one of the groups. They told them to create a **concept map** which consisted of many nodes.

On each node, the participants would write one of their many identities, for example, parent, lawyer, cyclist, etc. The identities didn't have to be relevant to the test.

Here's how it looked:

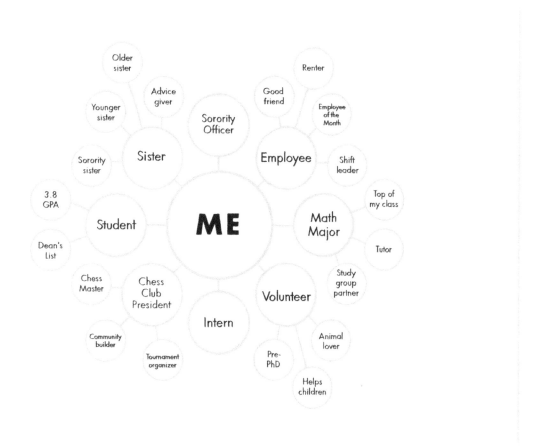

After reviewing the results of the tests, the researchers concluded that **the group that drew a concept map was able to fight the Stereotype Effect because they recalled they are multidimensional beings with a variety of attributes.**

The group that wasn't told to create a concept map underperformed as expected.

You can use this knowledge both on yourself and others.

For now, flip to the next page to create your concept map.

Your Concept Map.

Identities And Environment

As Doctor Rosenbloom learned more about these studies, he realised that identities can become more or less powerful according to the environment they happen to be under at each moment.

In simple terms, Rosenbloom "became" a doctor when he went to his office and wore his medical coat.

At the same time, his "patients" had to fall into that identity, which also meant that they were forced to listen to the expert.

Your turn: What are some identities you adopt, and are connected to a specific environment?

Environment	Identity/Identities
Home	-Father -Husband

Shared Identities

This has been a "Who are we?" conversation all along. But how can we connect with others when their identity clashes with ours?

How could Doctor Rosenbloom connect with his patients? How can a mature parent connect with their rebellious teenage son or daughter?

The process is the following:

1. Ask questions.
2. Listen carefully to find out what identities are emerging during the conversation.
3. Reciprocate by opening up on that specific identity.

For Doctor Rosenbloom, as an example, this meant that he could potentially connect with his patients over the "parent" identity, focusing on reciprocating on the importance of making the right decisions for your children.

Once again, remember that this is going to help you connect with others, even though they might not necessarily change their mind.

Your turn: Planning ahead never hurt anyone. What are some shared identities you can use to connect with the important people in your life?

Connect With	Shared Identity/Identities

Chapter 7: How Do We Make The Hardest Conversations Safer?

This chapter is dedicated to making hard conversations easier when it comes to identities. The author provides a set of advice divided into 3 parts:

1. Questions to answer before a hard conversation.
2. What to do at the beginning of a hard conversation.
3. What to do during a hard conversation.

Before A Hard Conversation

Hard conversations can be uncomfortable, there is no way to work around that.

What you can do, however, is to **become more resilient toward that discomfort**. To achieve that, you need to do some work in advance.

On the next few pages, you will find a set of questions suggested by the author. Think of a hard conversation that you might need to have and answer the questions to better prepare for the discomfort so you can push through it when it's time.

What do you hope to accomplish with this conversation?

_____

_____

_____

_____

What do you think others hope to say and learn?

_____

_____

_____

_____

How will this conversation start?

_____

_____

_____

_____

What obstacles might emerge? Will people get angry?

_____

_____

_____

_____

How can you make it safer for everyone to air their thoughts?

_____

_____

_____

_____

When those obstacles appear, what's the plan? How will you calm yourself and others if the conversation gets tense?

_____

_____

_____

_____

What are the benefits of this dialogue?

_____

_____

_____

_____

How will you remind yourself and others why this dialogue is so important?

_____

_____

_____

_____

At The Beginning Of The Discussion

At the beginning of a hard conversation, it is important to announce the dialogue's guidelines in order to make sure that everyone is aware of them.

The following checklist will help you set the right frame:

- ☐ Explain the boundaries, what's accepted and what not. For example, don't use the word "retarded" because you are talking about a sensitive matter of mental disability.
- ☐ Acknowledge that there is going to be some discomfort and mistakes will happen. Some wrong things might be said unintentionally.
- ☐ The goal is to share, experiences and perspectives, not convince.
- ☐ No blaming, no shaming, no attacks.
- ☐ Speak about your own opinions and experiences, not things you heard.
- ☐ Confidentiality and respect for everyone and toward everyone.
- ☐ Recalling specific experiences may be re-traumatizing. Discomfort is expected but if trauma or pain occurs, that's a sign to pause.

During The Conversation

While a hard conversation is going on, you need to be alert. Here's what to keep in mind:

1. Keep an eye out for what sort of identities are emerging.
2. Make sure there is equality for everyone. For example, everyone gets time to speak in a group meeting, don't allow others to interrupt them, etc.
3. Acknowledge their experience. "I'm sorry you had to go through X".
4. Manage the environment. Do your best to create an environment where everyone (or just the other person) feels protected to open up.

Your turn: What are the measures you need to take for your hard conversation?

Ensuring Equality	Managing The Environment
Not being distracted by my phone so they feel they have my full attention.	*No alcohol or food around.*

You made it!
You've completed the exercise book.

Claim your free bonus

There's a free bonus waiting for you as thanks for picking up this exercise book. We think you'll like it. Inside, you'll find a list of the most impactful self development books from this year, including:

- Top books for self-growth and mindfulness
- Top books for financial growth
- Top books for relationships (including yourself)
- Top books for productivity and "Getting Things Done"

We hope they provide a little inspiration for you - and perhaps some new discoveries.

To get your free bonus, scan the QR code below or visit BigActionBooks.com/bonus.

Scan to get your free bonus

Would you help us with a review?

If you enjoyed the exercise book, we'd be so grateful you could help us out by leaving a review on Amazon (even a super short one!). Reviews help us so much - in spreading the word, in helping others decide if the exercise book is right for them, and as feedback for our team.

If you'd like to give us any suggestions, need help with something, or to find more exercise books for other self-development books, please visit us at BigActionBooks.com.

Thank you

Thank you so much for picking up the exercise book for Charles Duhigg's *Supercommunicators*. We really hope you enjoyed it, and that it helped you practise the lessons in everyday life.

Thanks again,
The Big Action Books team

Notes:

Notes:

Notes:

Notes:

Notes:

Made in United States
North Haven, CT
19 November 2024

60620154R00037